I0108699

HINTS TO MECHANICS.

LONDON :

PRINTED BY SAMUEL BENTLEY,

Dorset Street, Fleet Street.

HINTS TO MECHANICS,

ON SELF-EDUCATION
AND MUTUAL INSTRUCTION.

BY

TIMOTHY CLAXTON.

BIRTH-PLACE OF MECHANICS' INSTITUTIONS.—*See page* 195.

LONDON:
PRINTED FOR TAYLOR AND WALTON,
28, UPPER GOWER STREET.
1839.

PREFACE.

———

THE Author (as he may be considered) of the following work is unwilling that the appearance of his name in the title-page should be the means of gaining credit for himself which he does not deserve, or of depriving other parties of any which belongs to them. He therefore thinks it his duty—and he need not say it is a great pleasure also, to acknowledge his obligations to several individuals—most of them distinguished more or less as the friends of mechanics—in addition to others whose names may appear in connexion with the aid they have furnished in the course of the following pages. The Author feels, however, more particularly that it would not be right to omit especial mention of his friend, B. B. Thatcher, Esquire, of Boston, United States,—a gentleman heretofore long known to

him as well-informed and deeply interested in the
condition and welfare of mechanics; and who,
while recently in this country, has rendered him
most valuable assistance in the preparation of this
volume for the press.

The Author is the more impelled to be explicit
on this point from the character of his own education, as will appear in the memoir he has introduced. The inferences to be made from this nar-
rative are such, in regard to his qualifications in
book-making, that the reader probably will be
much less surprised at the acknowledgment he
now makes, than he would have been had the
Author suppressed this avowal of the credit which
is due to his friends.

A selection of Exercises is inserted at the end
of the book, for the benefit of the smaller institutions, as it frequently happens that considerable
difficulty is experienced by them in the selection
of suitable subjects for lectures and discussions.
And it may be remarked, that there is not one of
the useful arts, however humble, but would afford
matter for instruction and amusement, if treated
properly, in relation to its history, progress, and

present state ; and the same might be said of all the branches of science.

A list of institutions is added, which is far from being complete, though an attempt has been made by a printed circular to obtain a fuller list ; but from the isolated state of the various institutions, and other causes, it is a difficult matter. The Author will continue his exertions, however, and at some future period a more complete list may appear : he therefore solicits information in relation to them, and to any other subjects connected with the moral and intellectual improvement of mechanics.

TIMOTHY CLAXTON.

46, Mary Street, Hampstead Road, London.
November 29, 1838.

CONTENTS.

CHAPTER I.

CHAPTER II.

CHAPTER III.

CHAPTER IV.

CHAPTER V.

HINTS TO MECHANICS.

CHAPTER I.

THE AUTHOR'S PURPOSE. — INTRODUCTION OF HIM-
SELF. — CIRCUMSTANCES OF HIS EARLY LIFE. — OP-
PORTUNITIES.— USE OF THEM.— POVERTY AND HARD
WORK.—HINTS ABOUT "LUCK."—FIRST MONEY AND
FIRST BOOKS. — HELP IN OTHER WAYS. — PRO-
GRESS IN SELF-EDUCATION.— DRAWING AND OTHER
BRANCHES OF KNOWLEDGE.—SETS OFF FOR LONDON.
—PROCEEDINGS THERE.—A MECHANICS' INSTITUTION
FORMED IN 1817.—GOES TO RUSSIA.—TO AMERICA.
—ADVENTURES, OBSERVATIONS, AND HINTS.

ASSUMING the sort of authority which perhaps
I do in the title of this little work, as humble as
it is, I believe the best excuse I can offer for it to
my fellow mechanics, is to give them a brief account of who I am, and of the kind of life which I
have led. In this sketch I shall be able to furnish
some few of the *hints* by which I wish them to
profit; and at the same time they will see that it
is not wholly without experience on my own part
that I venture at the present stage of my career
to volunteer, in so public a manner, as the adviser
and the warm advocate of what I consider to be
the true interests of my fellow-workmen.

To proceed then to business at once. I was born in the year 1790, about a hundred miles from London, and one mile from a small market-town. My parents were poor, and, what is worse, uneducated; but, much to their credit, the embarrassment which they suffered themselves from want of education only opened their eyes the more to the importance of giving their children a better chance than they had themselves enjoyed. So, although there were five of us, and our labour was of some consequence to them, I (the third), at six years of age, was put to a school-master in the neighbouring market-town for two years, excepting harvest-time each season, when I was taken home to aid my industrious mother in gleaning, which, in that part of the country, is a great help to the poor.

This schooling was paid for by a benevolent lady, who, as long as she lived, kept six boys and six girls at school for two years each, one half of the children leaving every year to give place to new ones. I was chosen to fill the place of a lad who had played truant, and after three months' trial was given up for a dunce. I was then a year younger than that at which the boys were usually admitted. Once a year the teacher was required to parade us at the mansion of our generous patroness, where we underwent a sort of examination; she then inquired of those leaving the school what books they wanted, and in most cases had them ordered. After the ceremony was over each pupil was presented with a shilling, and all proceeded to another room, where a sumptuous dinner (as we thought it) was spread out, at which we were attended by the servants. At this school I learned my reading and writing, and advanced in arithmetic, in which I was rather quick, as far as the rule of three.

All this, certainly, was a great step gained; and I desire here to acknowledge what I owe to my patroness. It is remarkable how easily a person so disposed, with even much smaller means than this good lady had, may do a great deal of good, as well as produce much happiness, among her fellow-creatures. Perhaps some kind soul, who honours my humble memoir with a glance, may gather a *hint* even from this.

Others may say again, " Well, this was a mere piece of luck, and I hope the author takes no credit to himself for it, or for the fair start in his education and whole career, which he thus may be said to have secured." Certainly I *do*. Some good fortune there was in it, no doubt, as there was in my having parents who, though ignorant themselves, appreciated the importance of knowledge. And so there is *some* good fortune belonging to every man's situation: at least, I never knew a case where there was not. I never saw any circumstances, where there was *a disposition to make the best of them*, which were half so bad as they might be imagined to be. This making the best of one's self and one's circumstances is the main thing after all, as I mean to show more fully. "Where there's a will there's a way," is the old version of the same great truth. Perseverance, vigilance, diligence,— these are what we want.

As for me, I take credit for making the most of the opportunity I had. Whether the other children did, is another question; but everybody knows that opportunities are good for nothing excepting to those who use them aright. Besides, I have noticed,, even in the course of *my* life, that opportunities, some how or other, only fall to the lot of one sort of people. Your shiftless, loose fellows seldom meet with what is called *good luck*. It is your men who look out for opportunities, and know the worth of them, and are willing to work upon them accordingly, and who in fact deserve all the good they get by them; these are the men, or the boys, who meet with a great part of the *good luck* which I know or care much about. In other words, I believe little in any "gains without pains," as poor Richard has it ; and I agree also with him that " *Diligence is the mother of good luck*," and that " God gives all things to industry." I flatter myself I have never been without this merit, and it makes amends for the want of many other things. It generally brings friends among the rest. I believe I had a pretty good name for it, and for a disposition to learn, when I was selected for the good lady's school mentioned above. That was not *all* "good luck;" or, if it was, there are very few lads, however poor, who cannot be as lucky as I was. It depends on themselves: I mean, of course, it depends on themselves under Divine Providence. Let me always be understood on this point, and now once for all: When I commend my readers to what I consider a good course of life, it is with a primary view to the approbation of God: it is thus that I speak of good luck, it is thus I recommend industry, for example. In dustry is a means of success appointed by Providence. "God gives all things to industry," says Richard. It is thus that industry is sure of success; and so of every other good practice. This is a hint most important of all, and which I desire may not be forgotten.

My father was a day-labourer, and had now no particular work for me. I was set to spinning wool by hand for a year or more. Then I was released to take care of a flock of sheep, which I got very tired of, and was glad enough to engage in a garden for supplying the market, till I was near thirteen, when I was apprenticed. My father gave me the choice of being a carpenter or a whitesmith. I chose the latter, and have continued in that business, or kindred branches, now over thirty years. I was to serve seven years for certain weekly wages, and ten pounds were to be added at the end of the term if I was thought to deserve it. My father was to board me, the consequence of

which was that I had a mile to walk to my work.
We began at six in the morning, and left off at
seven in the evening,—on Saturday at six,—al-
lowing an hour and a half for meals.

In this place I soon found the use of my schooling (which is another hint). There were older
apprentices than myself; but they could none of
them take an account of the work delivered from
the shop: the foreman was glad to put this task
upon me, and I was quite as willing to do it. It
was a relief in my monotonous labour, and it gave
me a new *opportunity* of trying and improving my
powers. It was an advance, in fact, in my education as well as in my comfort; and having got once
fairly started at school, I was determined to take
every opportunity of making further progress by
myself which I could. I always admired the question of Edmund Stone, the great mathematician.
He was a son of the gardener of the Duke of
Argyle, and was seventeen years old, when his
Grace, walking over his grounds one day, noticed
Newton's *Principia* lying on the grass, and, suppos-
ing it his own copy, directed it to be taken to its
place. Stone appeared, and claimed it. " Yours!"
said the Duke; " do *you* understand geometry,
Latin, and Newton?"—" A little," answered the
boy. He was further questioned, and excited the
Duke's amazement still more. " And how came
you with all this?" he inquired at last. " A ser-
vant," said Stone, " taught me ten years since to

read. *Does any one need to know any more than the letters to learn everything else that he wishes ?"*

The apprentices were sometimes called on, when our employer was absent, to aid in his sale-shop (ironmongery); and here was another opportunity for us. I could see something of the world here, and of a new description of business, and I am one of those who believe in the policy of keeping our eyes and our ears open in whatever situation we are. Be assured, brother mechanic, there's nothing like observing and thinking, and doing things for one's self. Here lies the great difference between men. This is the way to get the best education in the world: I would not give a fig for one to be had in any other.

In the workshop itself there was a great variety of work done; we made or repaired nearly every article of metal which is used in or about a house, together with mechanics' tools, and some work for mills. Here was a tolerable scope for the abilities of us young men.

The first money I received—ever received, I may say—was at Christmas, having then the privilege of calling on my master's customers for the usual " box." I got about half a guinea in this way, and I spent it in a new Bible, containing the Apocrypha, and a good thick cyphering-book. Soon after I began my arithmetic anew by myself, going through it much more thoroughly than at school. Here I made very decent progress, and I

have felt the benefit of it ever since. I might, to
be sure, have excused myself from extra labour,
after working ten or eleven hours for my employer.
Some apprentices of my acquaintance, in circumstances like my own, did so; and some do so still.
It is very common for them, and for older workmen, to complain of want of time. For my part, I
never yet knew the mechanic who could plead the
excuse with justice. I never knew one who had
not time enough for *other things*, more palatable to
him than the improvement of his mind, and the
advancement of his education. I never knew one
who could not find time occasionally, not to say
every evening, for indulging some worse than useless appetite or habit, or for mixing in society ill
calculated to do him any real good. But of this
hereafter; meanwhile let it pass for a *hint*. " Dost
thou love life?" Poor Richard asks : " then squan-
der not *time*, for that is the stuff life is made of."
Dost thou love money, leisure, ease, friends, respect, influence, a good conscience, good health, or
a good name? let me add; why, then, lose not
time; use it well. It is a sure way of getting all
these good things, and there is no other.

That I acted strictly on this principle myself I
do not pretend. I am far from making myself a
model in any respect. But sometimes we may do
as much good by warning a friend against our own
example, as by advising him to follow it. However, I was not an idler. I neither squandered

much time, nor overlooked many opportunities;
and there is something, by the way, in seeing
sharply what opportunities one has (I have already
said that everybody has them, more or less), and
in seizing upon them, and making the most of
them, *at the time.* " Many a mickle makes a muc-
kle," and, " a bird in the hand is worth two in the
bush," are proverbs I have learned since then; but
I had heard people say, *"every little helps,"* and
that was good English for me. I sought advice
and aid in my studies from everybody who came
in my way. I remember particularly a journeyman
carpenter who helped me much. He had a great
treasure, as it was *then,* in several books full of
examples in mensuration of superficies and solids,
embracing the methods of measuring various kinds
of artificers' work. I had evening lessons from this
man for awhile; but, unhappily, he died soon after
I began them, and the books were bought of his
widow by his employer,—a great numskull, so ignorant, that when a lady wrote to him to make her
a pheasant-house of an " hexagonal" form, he beset
my poor friend Tom, the journeyman, for a week
or two, to ascertain what the word meant. Evi-
dently he believed nobody but Tom could give
him this information. He did not know enough
to know where to look for *more,* but without
doubt he had a dim notion that, by buying
Tom's books, he should somehow succeed to his
knowledge.

The decease of the journeyman, and the departure of his books, were heavy afflictions to me; but I did not despair. I did not even give up mechanical drawing; in which, by perseverance and the circumstances of facilities increasing as I grew older, I made very good proficiency, much to my benefit in after life. I did something also in the ornamental branch of the art.

Another thing, which I then practised, has been of the greatest service to me since. My father could neither read nor write; he liked, however, to hear us children read, and we had always a lesson in the Scriptures after dinner on the sabbath. But, what was luckiest for me, he had letters to write, —that is, to *send*,—and most of these fell to me. At first, he dictated for me, word by word; afterwards he gave me a general notion of what he wanted, and left the filling-up to my discretion. I even did something of the sort now and then for a neighbour. The *practice*, if I got nothing else by it, was all gain to me. To this day I feel the benefit of the confidence and readiness which it gave me: deficient as I still am, I have a freedom in committing my thoughts to paper which would have repaid me for ten times the pains which I took to obtain it. It is like feeling at ease to converse in private society, or to speak at a public meeting, or to mingle pleasantly and comfortably in general with our fellow-creatures in all situations. These all come, in a great measure, by practice; and all help a man greatly *to make the best of himself.* They give him not only comfort, but influence and respect, and access to continually-opening facilities. Nor is there a mechanic living who might not often profit materially,—to say not a word of pleasure,—from the possession of a due measure of that just and manly confidence arising from the knowledge of his powers, either in writing or speaking, which a little drilling will give him. I know it comes hard at first to some: it did to me. But that is no reason for giving up in despair at the first effort, as I have known some do, through a miserable false shame. " There is nothing to be had, worth getting, without hard work," is an old saying; and " labour *will* do anything," is another. You know the history of the great orator Demosthenes, and what a bungling business he made of it when he began. The late celebrated dissenting minister, Robert Hall, made as sad a failure of it in the pulpit at first.

Nor let any mechanic tell me he has no *talent.* If I or anybody else were to tell *him* so, he would be offended. He might as well tell me he has no *time.* Let him use what he has, as he ought to do, and I will guarantee the result. At any rate, he cannot say what his abilities are *without trying*, and should he find himself really rather slow, why, all I have to add, by way of a *hint,* is, so much the more need he has of making the most of what talent he *has!* " By diligence and patience the mouse ate in two the cable," says Poor Richard. " Keep moving," brother mechanic.

The reader must not suppose my studies were all
theoretical, or literary. I had a strong taste for
mechanical pursuits, and spent a good deal of time
in divers curious experiments ;—some sketch of a
few of them may serve, at least, to amuse the
reader. I will say, however, that they were not a
mere amusement to me: they gave me that freedom of handling, inventing, and improving, in ma-
nual pursuits, which is of course all-important to
any mechanic, and wherein,—just as was said above
of writing and speaking, — the more drilling he
gives himself, the better. Besides, they induced
me to think, inquire, understand, reason, and remember a good deal more than I should other-
wise have done. I am convinced, on the whole, it
was much better than going into bad company, or
moping of an evening in the chimney-corner.

My master-piece, perhaps, was a clock. The
death of my friend gave me an opportunity to pur-
chase a small bench-vice, and some other tools, of
his widow. I made myself a small lathe, chiefly of wood, and several other tools, before I commenced with my clock. It was in the examination
of a large church clock, that my attention was first
drawn to this subject ; the wheels being large, it
looked much more simple than a common clock.
The principal difficulty which I apprehended was in
the motions necessary for the hands, where some of
the axes pass through the others. The materials to
which I had access were not very suitable for the

work; however, I began operations. It will be understood that, as I lived so far off, my meals were taken in the shop, my mother putting what was necessary for me to take every morning into a small basket. This plan gave me considerable time to prepare those parts at the shop which I could not do so well at home. (My master never expressed any objection to my amusing myself in this way: in fact, he did not trouble himself about it.) I prepared two plates of sheet-iron for the frame; these were kept at a suitable distance apart by four pieces of iron wire, which were riveted into the back-plate; the front plate was moveable. These plates were bushed with brass wherever it was necessary for the pivots of the several axes to pass through them. This, in point of utility, was as well as though the plates had been made wholly of brass. The wheels were of sheet brass, cut from the bottoms of old kettles. It was too thin, but was the best I could get. Having prepared my wheels, and fastened them on pieces of wire, the turning, dividing, and cutting the teeth, were performed at home.

I often smile to think of the scene presented when I first began. It was winter-time; my mother was sitting on one side of the fire, and the other was occupied by some members of the family. It being very cold, that side of the table farthest from the fire was vacant. Here I screwed my vice, and pinched my lathe in the vice, putting the axle, with the wheel on it, between the dead centres of the lathe. The motion was given by a drill-bow, the string of which passed round a whirl placed temporarily on the axis. The bow was moved by the left hand, while the tool was held firmly in the right. In this manner the wheels, pinions, and pivots were all turned ; the dividing was done by a pair of small spring-dividers, and the teeth were formed with a file. Parts of the work required hammering. This was more than some of the family could endure ; and it induced them to furnish me with a separate light, and I had to decamp. I found a place up stairs, screwed my vice to the bannister-rail, and, with a piece or two of board, I formed a bench, and was now fixed for the winter. In the following summer I made a much better establishment in a shed in the yard, where I completed my task, to the wonder of all the old women in the neighbourhood, but not exactly to my own satisfaction, although I thought it was as well as could be expected, taking all the circumstances' into consideration. It kept time tolerably well, and would show the hour and minute on the front dial. It had also an hour-hand on each side, which I had never seen before, although I had heard of it. The weight moved only thirteen inches, and required winding up once in about four and a half days.

It is impossible for any one who has never tried it, to conceive what pleasure there is in attempts of this kind, especially when the mind marks out tracks that have never been trodden before. Sometimes months, and even years must elapse, before the object of our pursuit can be brought to an issue, during which time there is a strong belief that the thing can be accomplished, although many unforeseen difficulties occur, which set us to thinking. Here is something to study about. Now and then a faint ray of light seems to point out the course we ought to pursue; after a while a blaze bursts, as it were, upon us, and the object can now be accomplished with ease. This brings pleasure somewhat in proportion to the labour spent in searching for it; or according to the benefit likely to arise to mankind, or to the individual making the discovery,—modified, of course, by the disposition of the person engaged in the operation. Frequently I have been bent upon the accomplishment of some object that required great attention, which I found was more easily done in the night, when the family had retired to rest, and all around was still. At such times, sleep would be banished from my eyes, there being something so fascinating in my pursuit, that the hours flew unconsciously by, and I retired to bed, rather for a screen to prevent the interference of others, than for the sake of rest.

My holidays, I need hardly say, were always welcome, though not as to most of my associates. I could study and work more of a holiday than in several evenings together.

"Well, I served out my apprenticeship "duly and truly." My master gave me ten pounds with my indenture, and asked me what I should do with myself. "Go to London, sir," answered I, for I had made up my mind. "Well, Tim," said he, "keep your right hand forward, and you will do well enough;" and he gave me a hearty farewell.

I reached this great city in April, 1810. From the circumstance of having lived in a rural district, I had then never seen so much as a steam-engine, or heard a lecture on anything, or read a book connected with the arts and sciences, save what I have mentioned, and a poor geography borrowed for a short time. The reader will bear these things in mind. He must make allowances for the generation of mechanics of that day, which are not to be made for those of this. A man, or a boy, then, might possibly talk with some plausibility of the lack of opportunities. Nothing had then been done to cheapen, and circulate, and simplify useful knowledge for the mass of the people. There were no Mechanics' Institutions— no popular libraries or reading rooms—no lectures which we operatives could get at, or understand if we did. A worthy printer, largely engaged in useful publications, lately said, in giving evidence before a committee of the House of Commons, "It is a great satisfaction to consider that we set three hundred and sixty thousand of these works in circulation every Saturday morning." Satis-

faction indeed! But there was no such thing *then*,
— no Family Libraries — no Penny Magazines.
There was not so much as a coffee-room, suitable
for a mechanic, in all London, when I entered it.
The first was established, where it still remains,*
in 1811, whereas there are now over one thousand,
besides two thousand eating-houses, in all which
these publications are to be had gratis by the customers, in addition to the great economy which
they are enabled by these establishments to prac-
tise in other respects, to say nothing of the snug
comfort and decent society which most of them
supply. For a London mechanic, especially, to
talk now-a-days of having no chance to improve
his mind or his manners is the merest nonsense in
the world. He has hardly a chance to avoid it.
He must almost be a decided sot, a glutton, a
gambler, a thief, or an idiot, to do so.

Of course the metropolis was full of novelty for
me. But I had business in hand, and went about
it. I soon got work; and here I will remark that
I have never, from that day to this, in any city or
country, been without it, save when I travelled for
my own pleasure or improvement; nor do I believe much in the necessity of a mechanic, in tolerable health, being destitute at any time of regular
employment. I had leisure on my hands at first,
and knowing there was really a vast deal to be

* Potter's Original Coffee-House, 35 High-street, Blooms-
bury, facing the east end of Oxford Street.

learned in London, I spent much of it in going about, seeing what there was to be seen. After a while I became a more settled character again. I bought a lathe and some other things; and among the rest, last though not least, I got a wife to assist me. So, having a home once more, and feeling " at ease in my possessions," I went to drawing again, which I found the cheapest pastime I knew of, besides that it sharpened my observation, and aided my understanding and memory. Many trades cannot be carried on without it, and I consider it extremely serviceable to *all* mechanics. The apparatus, too, makes very little noise or dirt, takes up little room, and can be readily got out, packed away, or carried about.

Another affair which I engaged in I shall mention, rather at my own expense; but it furnishes a *hint*, and so no matter. I was in a large machine-shop, with workmen from all quarters. In such places strange notions abound. With some of my associates it was "*perpetual motion,*"—that everlasting nonsense and nuisance to so many ingenious but ill-informed men,—for I suppose it clear enough that no truly well-instructed mechanic would waste any time and thought about it. And yet what multitudes have wasted months and years, all for the want of that decent information in the plain principles of practical science which would have shown them the absurdity of the thing on its face. I confess I laboured under the delusion myself, and no wonder, for it was quite a disorder with many at the time. My first attempt was to make the descending side of a wheel heavier than the ascending side, by causing moveable parts to approach and recede from its centre; but let me modify it how I would, there always were a greater number of those moveable parts on the ascending side, so that, although they were made to recede farther from the centre after passing the top, they were fewer in number on the descending side, and the wheel would turn as well backwards as forwards. Many other methods were tried, and some of them with fluid matter. A syphon was made with the short leg much larger than the long one, that it might contain a greater weight of water, and over-balance that in the long leg; but I found it was necessary that the discharging end should be lower than the surface of the water in the vessel, what-ever might be the form of the syphon.

But let this nonsense pass; I have referred to it only as a warning to other young fellows, and because it gives me occasion to remind my readers — and this their own experience, I dare say, has done long since — of the infinity of time, thought, talent, and spirits, worse than lost and wasted, every day that we live, by multitudes of mechanics in all directions around us, not in "perpetual motion" altogether, but in various schemes on the same principle — that is, on no principle at all; and which a decent knowledge of real principles, such as they all ought to learn, and might as well as not, would at once have taught them to despise and reject. If there were no other use in education or information to a mechanic, but this alone of keeping him to his own business, I should say it is worth any cost at which he can get it. This ignorance operates in a hundred ways; but I cannot go into details here. I have seen many persons much given up, on account of it, to very silly superstitions. Quacks of all sorts find their fit prey in such characters. Many of them are found coming out with *patents*. We see a good deal of this in England, but the Americans have more of it, (though a very intelligent people generally,) because the cost of getting a patent out is so trifling under their laws. There are advantages in this, but it encourages a sorry waste of time among foolish schemers. I believe full five-sixths of the enormous number of patents taken out in the United States, hitherto, have been of no earthly use whatever but to make a laughing-stock of the inventors. The American patent-law, however, has been altered, and a commissioner appointed to examine the various claims for patents, which I am glad to perceive has had the effect of reducing the number of useless ones. In 1837 about one-third of the applications were rejected, and the right of appeal had not in a single case been exercised.

For my own part I would rather exhibit a mouse-trap of mine, the work of a few leisure evenings, for it had at least the merit of novelty, and I think of ingenuity as well. An acquaintance had made a box-trap for catching mice, and was showing it as a specimen of his ingenuity: " Now," said I, " if you had made it so that after the mouse was caught, he would set the trap ready for another, and then go and drown himself, it would have been worth something." He exclaimed, " That is impossible; that is more than you can do." I told him I would produce one in a fortnight's time. And so I did; and after that another more simple than the first. These mouse-traps were pronounced to be the greatest curiosities in my collection, which was considerable.

The first trap consisted of a box, open at one end, and a wire grating at the other. When the mouse entered the trap, and began nibbling the cheese, the door at which he entered would fall down. There was a hole in the side of the box, on pushing his way through which he raised the end of a lever, and started some clockwork placed on the top of the box, by which the trap was set again; while the noise of the wheels so startled the little fellow, that he would run up inside a spiral wire tube into a jar of water before he was aware of it. In the second trap, instead of the clock-work, it was set again by the mouse turning a hollow wheel like a squirrel-cage. It was so contrived that after entering this wheel, he must either work or stop there ; but the instant he set the trap, a little door opened on one side of the wheel, when he would escape from it, to be let down by a trap-door into the water. I preserve this gimcrack to the present day. It is worth all the perpetual motions I ever saw.

However, setting the mouse-trap aside, I come to the more important period of my life. I was just twenty-five years of age, when I saw for the first time a course of lectures announced. It was on Natural Philosophy and Chemistry. The talk about pneumatics, hydrodynamics, &c., was of course all Greek to me ; but looking farther down, I found notices of experiments to be made on engines, and so on, and so I bought a ticket, and attended the first lecture.   This pleased me so much that I took notes, and also drew sketches of the apparatus (where my old practice came in play, you perceive). Going home, I sat up very late to write out all I could remember of the lecture ; and here my juvenile practice helped me again, even the tiresome copying I used to do for my father. So I went on, from October 1815 till the next April. Then I got a book on Natural Philosophy, and followed the subject up, for there's nothing, I found, like " *striking while the iron is hot.*" Then I made various articles to try experiments with, which my mechanical practice rendered easy work. I went to a second course, and then to others given by other persons.

Finally, I applied for admission to a Philosophical Society; but, alas! one wanted friends at court in those days. Never discouraged, however, what should I do in such a case? Let any mechanic of this generation imagine himself living twenty years ago, and consider. "Why," thought I, "I am *a mechanic*, and though that is the very reason why I wish to be admitted, and why I should be, it is the very reason, also, why I am not." It is clear, then, the mechanics must look to themselves, and to each other. Well, a number of us having talked it over, I wrote a circular, dated June 24th, 1817, (it was well I could write one,) got it printed, and sent it round town. From this paper I make the following liberal extract, for I think it worthy of being put on record, and, indeed, something of a curiosity, as it will be seen that even at this early date, six years before the London Mechanics' Institution was formed, and when none of us had even heard of what had been done at Glasgow, or elsewhere, the circular, nevertheless, embraces substantially all the important principles recognized by modern Mechanics' Institutions :—

" A few mechanics having associated themselves together for the purpose of establishing a Society of Ingenious Working Mechanics of all descriptions, provided they are respectable men, of good character, and a studious disposition, wish for a few intelligent persons to step forward and assist them in forming a Committee, and composing a set of Rules and Regulations for the conducting of a Society, which has for its object the study and improvement of the arts of this kingdom.

" We are well aware that there already exist many valuable societies for the promotion of the arts, but they do not seem to be adapted to the capacity of a working mechanic; we do not mean as to their terms of admission, or subscription afterwards, but the recommendation they require seems to be the grand obstacle, combined with the very scientific style of language and the *gentleman*-like appearance of their members; so that the class of people that compose those societies, and the class of people that we should wish to see possessed of the leading principles of the various branches of science, do not seem to have any inclination to associate together. The reason of this we cannot exactly determine upon; but it appears to be a sort of customary pride, that does not allow of the various degrees of men in high and low rank uniting in a body; and it may be very well it is so, as it obliges men who wish to set themselves forward in the world to endeavour to effect it by their meritorious exertions.

" By taking a view of the case in this light, it would seem advisable to form a Society a few degrees below those already in being, in order to make a path wherein the industrious tradesman may walk, and to give him an opportunity to improve the talents with which he is blessed; the advantages that would arise from the formation and proper conducting such a Society would be numerous.

" It is proposed to establish, by a moderate subscription, a Library of Books, chiefly of a scientific character, and likewise a Repository of Plans, Models of Machinery, and other works of art, for the inspection of the members.

" Such a Society would afford both rational and useful amusement, by attending once a week to hear a lecture on some useful branch of science, or the discussion of some question on mechanical or philosophical pursuits. It would create in us a mode of passing our leisure time in a way much preferable to what is already practised by too many,—it would make us better members of society,—better for ourselves, our employers, and consequently for our families."

The result of this appeal was, that a small Society was formed, which was called the *Mechanical Institution*, and continued in being for about three years. I began to move in this affair in 1816, but the Society was not organized till August of 1817, and it ceased to exist in 1820, on my going to Russia.

I performed the duty of secretary to this Society the whole of the time it existed, and am of opinion that its "decline and extinction" were owing, principally, to a want of taste for and experience in these matters. The meetings were held weekly, first in Brook's Market; then at the Compasses, High Holborn; and, lastly, at my house in Little Sutton-street, Clerkenwell. The exercises consisted of lectures and discussions on subjects relating to the arts and sciences, and sometimes social conversations on various subjects.

Not having a library of our own, we subscribed to Horne's celebrated library, (two guineas per annum, which allowed us about twenty volumes daily, though this was afterwards reduced to four volumes,) for the use of those members only who were engaged in the preparation of lectures. The rules, &c. of the Mechanical Institution were printed in a pamphlet form, and a notice of it given in the London Mechanics' Magazine, vol. xiv. page

446; it is thereby kept from oblivion, as it ought to be, for I am sure the efforts of several of its members deserved better success. The time, however, had not yet come for the mechanics to be sufficiently alive to their real interest, dignity, capacity, or wants. With some of them I fear it has not come even now.

The sequel of my memoir will be passed over lightly, for though I have seen something of the world, I do not wish to weary the reader with matters which do not concern him. In 1820, I went to St. Petersburg, where I remained three years, being engaged by the Emperor Alexander in putting up *gas-works.* Lord Bacon says, when we travel we should not adopt everything we see, but now and then " prick in a flower." Perhaps some *hints* may be had even of the Russian mechanics. We despise them in this country, but it does not follow that we thus show our wisdom. In many respects they are pretty well advanced. Their manufactories of iron, and of goods from hemp and flax, have been long celebrated. They have also carried the manufactories of paper, cotton, silk, and glass, to considerable perfection.

Granite is much used in their public works, for foundations of buildings, lining the canals and rivers, and for side-walks. Some of their columns made of granite are very large and highly polished. I took the pains to measure one of the columns intended for a new church, and found it fifty-six feet long, and near seven feet diameter at the base. They were brought from Finland, and two of them were a load for a ship, one on each side of the masts, to balance each other. They were rolled from the deck to the vicinity of the intended building on timbers nine inches square, (placed but little distance apart,) which were completely crush-ed to splinters. The rolling was performed by two ropes; one end of each being made fast, some dis-tance ahead, to stakes driven into the ground. They were passed under the column, up the back side, and over the top. The other end of each rope was wound round a separate capstan. Each capstan had four long levers, with from ten to twenty men at each lever. These columns were placed in a temporary building for polishing.

I also visited the foundry where the bases and capitals were made. They were of brass, of the Corinthian order, and highly polished and gilt. The square *plinth* for the bottom measured about nine feet on each side, and one foot thick. Seve-ral women and children were polishing these with pumice-stone. The *torus*, a round bead belonging to the base, was turning in the lathe, and the work-man had a very strong tool for this purpose. A steam-engine, with a man to attend it, was em-ployed entirely on the work. The capitals, with their leaves and volutes, had a very splendid ap-pearance.

The building in which I was engaged in putting up the gas-works, was for transacting the business of the Russian army. It was built in the form of a crescent, having a large arch in the centre, and was situated opposite the imperial palace. The area between these buildings was used as a parade-ground for the soldiers every morning. In this building were several departments, with a "general" at the head of each, some of whom employed above two hundred clerks. The library was very extensive, in the centre of which we put up a splendid chandelier, which cost 400*l.* sterling in England. It had three hundred and sixty jets of gas, issuing from a circle of brass seven feet in diameter, above which were four eagles lighted with gas. There was also a great quantity of richly cut glass about it. In this building I saw lithographic printing for the first time ; copper-plate and letter-press printing were carried on here, and a very extensive establishment for the manufacture of mathematical instruments, all belonging to the Government ; also a drawing-school, consisting of about two hundred young officers.

In another building I noticed a model of the machine on which a large block of granite, weighing upwards of nine hundred tons, was removed several miles. Peter the Great is said to have stood on this rock, giving commands to his army, when he subdued the Fins. The Empress Catherine ordered it to be removed to the city for a foundation on which to place a bronze statue of that monarch on horseback. Many ineffectual attempts were made for its removal; but it was easily performed afterwards by introducing cannon-balls for rollers between bars of iron.

I will *prick in* here three more " flowers," which some of my readers may be amused with, and possibly get a *hint* from.

Fig. 1.   Fig. 2.   Fig. 3.

 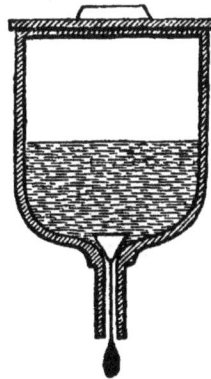 

Figure 1 represents a contrivance for shutting doors. The power is applied in the same manner as in our modern printing-presses. There is a pin at each end of the apparatus: one pin is fitted to and turns in a socket attached to the frame, and the other is fitted to a similar one on the door. In opening the door the pins are brought nearer together, and the weight in the centre is raised. The door is shut by this weight straightening the bars, and spreading the pins further apart. Some of these articles are made of iron, and are black; others are of brass, and kept bright; both kinds are extensively used. Figure 2 is a cistern for water, with a valve in the bottom, which is much used for washing the face and hands. By raising the valve the water is let down in small quantities, and, as it is used, passes off by means of a sink placed underneath. The advantages of this method are that persons do not wash in the same water with others, nor use it more than once themselves, which is not only more conducive to health, but makes less water necessary than washing in a common basin. These cisterns are made of various forms and sizes. Some of them have a dozen or more pipes, each furnished with a valve, so that many persons may wash at the same time; the large ones are made in a circular form, and placed in the middle of a room, but the small ones are hung against the wall. In figure 3 is represented a spring bow or arch. This is used with the horse-collar, for the horse that is placed in the shafts, as other horses do not have them. It was a long time before I could see any other use for this contrivance than to cause the horse to hold up his head, and to keep him from stumbling, by the bridle being hooked to the top of this arch. I was informed afterwards by an intelligent man, that the spring being connected with the collar prevented the shoulder of the animal from chafing, by continually easing the collar off, and suffering the air to pass between that and the shoulder of the horse.

I left Russia in 1823, and after a voyage of sixty-three days landed in Boston, America. I amused myself during the voyage, at such times as my health would permit, in the study of mathematics. I had previously made myself acquainted with the improved engineer's sliding-rule, and with decimal fractions, and committed to memory several useful factors, such as 3·1416, ·7854, 27·648, &c. These and many others were often used to find the superficial and solid contents, and also the weights of different bodies. After getting used to the motion of the ship, I commenced making a table, by which I might easily calculate the pressure of a column of water, of any diameter, and of any height. It began with a quarter of a foot, and was continued to several hundred feet high. Before it was finished, however, I perceived several repetitions; for the very same figures occurred in different answers; and on examining a little farther, I found out the rule by which they were governed, namely, shifting the decimal point, which enabled me to simplify my work very much. I found that the answers to the first nine numbers would answer for all the others, whether above or below unity; and there is no limit to this but our powers and our wants; for if we start with a millionth part of a unit, and continue to many millions of units, skipping only a millionth part at a time, we are still far within its limits; and yet this can be done within a small space, for the table that I first prepared took up many times the room of the improved one, although it was much more limited. I was highly delighted with this discovery; and, as it happened when I had several weeks of leisure, with very little to engage my attention, I pursued the subject with ardour, and before I left the ship several tables for various purposes were prepared.

Let me remark here how a decent degree of information, with habits of self-improvement, are worth getting, were it only to amuse one's self at times when all other sources of amusement fail.

Not to be tedious,—after a few weeks of looking about, I engaged to work in a machine-shop at a cotton-factory, situated something less than thirty miles from Boston, where I remained three years, commencing in the middle of September, 1823. Six months passed away without my being able to do anything towards my favourite object. In the spring of 1824, however, an opportunity offered for me to attempt the formation of a society for mutual improvement. Two discourses were delivered on a fast-day by the minister of the village : that in the afternoon was on the importance of knowledge, and the facility with which it can be obtained, by a judicious arrangement of our time, and our associating together for mutual benefit. In fact he expressed my views on the subject so well that I felt confident of a kind reception, and accordingly waited on him the same afternoon. After stating my views, and presenting him some papers on the subject, I was informed that a small Society for reading had existed about five years in the village, but was at a very low ebb at that time. He was pleased with my proposals, and invited me to attend the next meeting of the Society. I attended, and found a considerable number of both sexes assembled at the house of one of the members. They were engaged in reading by turns from Whelply's Compend of General History, and the president put questions to them as they proceeded, which made it interesting.

At the close of this exercise, he asked me how I liked it. "Very well," was the reply. I then inquired what other exercise they had. He told me that was all, excepting an annual address, which he delivered himself. I asked him if it would not be well to try the debating of questions, and familiar lectures on science and the arts. He said he thought well of it, but they felt very cautious how they ventured from the shore, lest they should get into deep water. I told him I thought they need not be afraid, for I had seen persons engaged in such exercises, whose opportunities for intellectual culture were inferior to theirs. I was asked if I could give them a lecture. I said I would try, and prepared myself accordingly. I had brought a small air-pump from Russia with me, which I made of a piece of gas tubing, with a ground-plate on a mahogany stand. I bought a few glass articles, which were ground to fit the pump plate, with a little sand and water, on the hearth-stone of my room. I also procured a small wash-tub, and fitted a shelf to it for a pneumatic cistern. In this way I succeeded with a very simple apparatus in explaining the mechanical and some of the chemical properties of the air.

This put new life into the Society: its constitution was revised so as to include a library and apparatus. Debating was also adopted with success, and the ladies handed in compositions, which were read at the meetings. The reading exercise was pursued only occasionally. Several of the members who had not studied any particular branch of knowledge were prevailed on to give lectures on subjects connected with their professions. More than one case occurred, however, in which gratitude was felt by those who had been thus roused into action.

The Society continued to meet at the members' houses until it became too large to be thus accommodated. They then tried the school-house, and the hall at the tavern; but not being satisfied with these, they built a two-story building for their accommodation, at an expense of twelve hundred dollars. The building was completed within two years from the time in which I was first introduced to the Society. The hall was let to another Society, and there were two mechanics' shops under the hall.

I left this place to reside in Boston in October, 1826, and have not visited it since, but have frequently been gratified by favourable accounts in relation to the prosperity of the Society.

On my arrival in Boston, the very first business I attended to was to make inquiries respecting mechanics' societies, and was surprised to find that no society existed to which a mechanic could go and hear lectures on subjects calculated to aid him in his vocation. There had been some talk of building a mechanics' hall, &c.; but that project was abandoned. I conversed with several persons on the subject, who were willing to assist in forming a society for mutual improvement. I put a notice into a newspaper, stating where names would be received, and finally called a meeting, which was attended by nine persons, and a second meeting, which was attended by only seven. At this meeting it was determined to make the thing more popular, by advertising in the daily papers, and hiring a hall in a central situation. The next meeting was held at " Concert Hall," and was very well attended. The result was the formation of the Boston Mechanics' Institution.

This Society soon became very popular, which induced others to imitate the example thus set. By this it was evident that in Boston, as well as other places, it only required a little exertion, on the part of those who felt an interest in the subject, to induce a portion at least of the citizens to improve their advantages.

The Massachusetts Charitable Mechanics' Association was next in the field. Soon after this, meetings were held to form a " Lyceum adapted to the city." Several plans were offered, but none of them met with general approbation. The consequence was, a division took place. One party formed the Society for the Diffusion of Useful Knowledge, while the other formed the Boston Lyceum. Since that time, several minor societies have been formed, not to mention the Franklin Lectures, which have been got up particularly for the accommodation of mechanics: so that Boston is now well supplied with societies for the improvement of the mind.

I have now given an account of myself, as far as proposed. If I have gone into details at some length, it was where I considered principles to be involved which could be best illustrated and enforced in that way. These principles, in my opinion, are of the first importance, especially to mechanics. They save and make money, character, reputation, and comfort; and what is more, they may just as well be adopted in practice as not ; and just as well by one man or boy as another. Indeed it is much easier working by principle on all occasions and subjects, than from mere habit, drilling, memory, whim, or chance. The waste a man makes in these ways is inconceivable, and he enjoys, and can enjoy, at the same time, no pride of independence, or self dependence, — no sense of ability of his own,—no satisfaction in the thought of being always ready for what may happen out of the beaten track,—no consciousness of mind developed and disciplined, of duty discharged, of difficulties conquered, or of success attained in his enterprises.

Of all these, I feel that I *have* had my share, and I desire ardently that my fellow-mechanics, one and all, may put themselves, early and late, in the way of securing the same results. I desire it the more, because I know by experience that it is in the power of them all to do so. It is not by any particular talent or genius which I pretend to, that I have done what I have done, and am what I am. Neither is it by any unusual good fortune, as I have shown. I could show, if necessary, that I have had my share of *bad*, being burnt out, and losing most of my stock and tools, by which my business was deranged for two months, and my library and private papers destroyed; but this is nothing to the purpose. The fact is,—and this is the one grand principle running through my little memoir, —every man is an artificer, good or bad. He is the maker *of his own fortune*. More of this by-and-by.

www.ingramcontent.com/pod-product-compliance
Lightning Source LLC
Chambersburg PA
CBHW081527040426
42447CB00013B/3368